An Evaluation of the Military OneSource Call Center in Select Groups of Callers

Call Quality, Call Outcomes, and Caller Satisfaction

ERIKA LITVIN BLOOM, LISA H. JAYCOX, THOMAS E. TRAIL,
ALLYSON D. GITTENS, GRACE GAHLON, STEVEN R. DICKERSON,
AMMARAH MAHMUD

Prepared for the Deputy Assistant Secretary of Defense
for Military Community and Family Policy
Approved for public release; distribution unlimited

 NATIONAL DEFENSE RESEARCH INSTITUTE

For more information on this publication, visit **www.rand.org/t/RRA1039-1**.

About RAND

The RAND Corporation is a research organization that develops solutions to public policy challenges to help make communities throughout the world safer and more secure, healthier and more prosperous. RAND is nonprofit, nonpartisan, and committed to the public interest. To learn more about RAND, visit www.rand.org.

Research Integrity

Our mission to help improve policy and decisionmaking through research and analysis is enabled through our core values of quality and objectivity and our unwavering commitment to the highest level of integrity and ethical behavior. To help ensure our research and analysis are rigorous, objective, and nonpartisan, we subject our research publications to a robust and exacting quality-assurance process; avoid both the appearance and reality of financial and other conflicts of interest through staff training, project screening, and a policy of mandatory disclosure; and pursue transparency in our research engagements through our commitment to the open publication of our research findings and recommendations, disclosure of the source of funding of published research, and policies to ensure intellectual independence. For more information, visit www.rand.org/about/principles.

RAND's publications do not necessarily reflect the opinions of its research clients and sponsors.

Preface

The Office of the Deputy Assistant Secretary of Defense for Military Community and Family Policy within the U.S. Department of Defense (DoD) administers the suite of services provided by Military OneSource, including a call-in service that provides free assistance and referrals to service members and their families 24 hours a day, 365 days of the year. Calls to the center are answered by trained triage consultants who provide information and/or connect callers to DoD and civilian programs and services that can help them cope with the challenges of military life. This report provides the findings of the RAND National Defense Research Institute's (NDRI's) analysis of call quality, call outcomes, and caller satisfaction within select groups of callers requested by the sponsor. Specifically, we conducted two studies. First, we reviewed audio recordings of calls and rated them on several dimensions, including the quality of the communication between the caller and the Military OneSource triage consultant, the outcome (e.g., was a referral made?), and caller satisfaction. Second, we conducted qualitative telephone interviews with a separate sample of callers in which we asked them to describe and rate their satisfaction with their experience in speaking to the Military OneSource consultants and with the referrals, services, or resources they received. As requested by the sponsor, Study 1 (the call ratings analysis) included (1) junior enlisted service members and their families, (2) those calling about a relationship problem, and (3) transitioning service members and their families. We intended to include callers from the same three groups in Study 2 (telephone interviews), but we were unable to include transitioning service members and had to expand the relationship problems group to callers who were seeking non-medical counseling for any issue. The sponsor approved of these changes to the eligibility criteria for the interview sample.

The report should be of interest to program leaders, who can use its findings as a benchmark for call quality and caller satisfaction and to identify opportunities for strengthening how triage consultants process calls. However, the results should be interpreted with some significant caveats and limitations in mind. The call ratings analysis only examined a small sample of calls from specific groups of particular interest to program leadership and RAND NDRI did not have control over the selection of calls for inclusion in the study. Similarly, the interviews only assessed a small, self-selected sample of callers from limited groups that differed somewhat from the call ratings analysis sample, so their experiences are not likely to be representative of all callers.

The research reported here was completed in January 2020 and underwent security review with the sponsor and the Defense Office of Prepublication and Security Review before public release.

This research was sponsored by the Office of the Deputy Assistant Secretary of Defense for Military Community and Family Policy and conducted within the Forces and Resources Policy Center of the National Security Research Division, which operates the National Defense Research Institute (NDRI), a federally funded research and development center sponsored by the Office of the Secretary of Defense, the Joint Staff, the Unified Combatant Commands, the Navy, the Marine Corps, the defense agencies, and the defense intelligence enterprise.

For more information on the RAND Forces and Resources Policy Center, see www.rand.org/nsrd/frp, or contact the director (con-tact information is provided on the webpage).

Contents

Figures and Tables

consent document to review. Participants provided verbal consent prior to beginning the interview, which lasted 15–30 minutes.

Results

Forty callers were interviewed: ten male service members, 11 female service members, and 19 female spouses of service members. Twenty-nine interviewees were seeking a referral for non-medical counseling (19 for individual counseling, and ten for relationship counseling); other reasons for calling included My Career Advancement Account (MyCAA) and/or school issues (six), document translation services (two), and other types of benefits, such as seeking childcare (three).

Overall, interviewees conveyed that were very satisfied with their experience in communicating with Military OneSource triage consultants. They described the consultants as friendly, supportive, helpful, and knowledgeable about military life. They liked that Military OneSource was free, fast (with regard to how quickly consultants answered the phone and connected them to resources and services), easy to use, available everywhere at all times, and private. Additionally, most interviewees said they were connected to the resources or services they were seeking and that they were satisfied with the help they received from these resources or services. One suggestion was to send callers an email summary of what was discussed, including contact information for any referred counselors or services, after the call. A few interviewees experienced delays or other problems in getting help but did not necessarily fault the Military OneSource triage consultant.

Some interviewees who were seeking non-medical counseling expressed that they would have preferred to receive a list of counselors and contact counselors on their own instead of being connected during a three-way call. Other general suggestions from interviewees seeking non-medical counseling included keeping the counselor list more up to date (i.e., making sure all counselors on the list are currently accepting new referrals from Military OneSource); providing more information about counselors (e.g., their type of degree/credentials/license, their specialty areas); and increasing the number of counselors that accept referrals from Military OneSource.

Overall Summary and Limitations

Overall, the Military OneSource calls we rated were of high quality with regard to communication style and successful in referring callers to appropriate resources. Any problematic issues that were revealed in the ratings occurred among a small minority of callers, and program staff could assess whether these small issues were of concern. Similarly, most callers who were interviewed expressed that they were satisfied with their experience in communicating with Military One-Source triage consultants, were referred to resources and services that met their needs, and offered limited suggestions for changes to the referral process.

Limitations

Limitations of the call ratings analysis include the small sample of calls, making it unlikely they were fully representative of typical calls. Moreover, we did not have control over the audio recording selection, and thus it is possible that there was bias in selection. Specifically, the calls sampled may overrepresent high-quality calls and not be representative of a general sampling of calls. Similarly, a limitation of the interviews with callers was the small sample of interviewees, who were unlikely to be representative of all callers. It is possible that callers perceived to be dissatisfied might not have been asked to participate in the study, might not have agreed to be contacted, or might have decided not to schedule an interview. Correspondingly, the caller rate of agreement to be contacted for the interview study is unknown, and most callers who agreed to be contacted did not follow up to schedule an interview, so we cannot assess the potential bias in selection for participation. Both studies (call ratings and caller interviews) looked across call centers and triage consultants and did not examine differences among these locations and individuals, possibly obscuring important variations in call quality. Also, in both studies, subgroups (e.g., junior enlisted service members, and those who called about a relationship problem) overlapped, and neither study was designed or intended to evaluate subgroup differences. Finally, we were not able to measure follow-up on the referrals offered, or how satisfied the callers were with these referrals and the help provided on a longer-term basis, as interviews occurred within a month after the call. Follow-up surveys or interviews would be necessary to understand whether the calls ultimately helped caller with their stated problems.

Acknowledgments

We would like to thank Cathy Flynn, Maia Hurley, Lee Kelley, Tricia Morzenti, Erika Slaton, and Towanda Street from the Office of Military Community and Family Policy for their guidance and support throughout the project. We also greatly appreciate the staff at ValueOptions for their efforts to transfer data to the RAND Corporation and assist with recruitment for the interviews, as well as military service members and their families who volunteered their time to participate in interviews. We must acknowledge the efficient and organized work of Francisco Walter from RAND in managing interview recruitment and scheduling, which was critical to the successful completion of the project. Finally, we thank Marek Posard from RAND and Deborah Bradbard from Syracuse University, who served as peer reviewers for this report and provided thoughtful feedback and recommendations.

Abbreviations

DoD	Department of Defense
FY	fiscal year
MC&FP	Military Community and Family Policy
MyCAA	My Career Advancement Account
NDRI	National Defense Research Institute
PTSD	posttraumatic stress disorder
SECO	Spouse Education and Career Opportunities

CHAPTER ONE

Background

The Military OneSource call center is an information and referral service funded by the U.S. Department of Defense (DoD) that serves as a central hub for providing information and connecting service members and their families to resources across a broad range of areas. The call center is a free service available 24 hours a day, 365 days a year, to all active duty, National Guard, and reserve service members and their families. As of August 13, 2018, the service was expanded to include retired and honorably discharged service members and their families up to one year after separation from the military. The triage consultants staffing the call center connect callers to DoD and civilian services that help with military or transition-related issues. Some of those services are provided through Military OneSource—for example, nonmedical counseling to address short-term problems through solutions-based counseling—and other services are provided through consultant referrals to DoD or civilian programs. The Military OneSource call center is distinct from the military crisis line, a separate line to which urgent calls are directed.

The goals of this set of studies were to evaluate Military One-Source call quality, call outcomes, and caller satisfaction. Discussions with the sponsor clarified that the studies should be restricted to three groups of callers who were of particular interest. First were calls from junior enlisted service members in the E3–E5 pay grades, since calls from these pay grades were shrinking over time, and the Military Family Readiness Council has recommended better understanding of the needs of younger adults. The second group of interest comprised those calling about relationship problems, since these constitute a large portion of calls and often result in referrals to non-medical counseling. Finally, the sponsor asked for evaluation of calls from service members who recently transitioned to civilian life (within one year of having left the military), since the expansion of eligibility to transitioning service members was relatively recent and the quality of calls from this group had not yet been assessed.

Our evaluation included two separate studies. Study 1 rated call audio recordings from these three groups of interest (i.e., junior enlisted members, those calling about a relationship problem, and those recently transitioned out of the military) for communication quality, call outcomes, and caller satisfaction; Study 2 comprised interviews with callers about their experience with Military OneSource and the resources that they were directed to by triage consultants. Our original intention was to interview callers from the same three groups. However, we were unable to interview those who recently transitioned from the military due to anticipated delays in Office of Management and Budget approvals that would not fit within the project timeline. In addition, the case management system did not allow for identification of those calling about relationship problems, and thus we had to expand the interview eligibility to those who called seeking any type of non-medical counseling (individual or relationship) or a referral to the Healthy Relationships Program. The sponsor approved of these changes to the eligibility criteria for the interview study. These studies were designed to offer an indication of the effectiveness of the call center in helping service members and their families gain access to resources and build resiliency and readiness.

Military OneSource Standard Operating Procedures

Call Center Staffing

Calls to the Military OneSource call center are answered by trained triage consultants who are tasked with interacting with callers, judging the nature of their concerns (if they were not clear) and determining the appropriate assistance to provide. Calls to the center encompass simple requests for information (e.g., contact information for military resources); crisis calls involving duty to warn or mandated reporting situations (e.g., suicide threats); or requests that are not crisis related but involve inquiries into available resources (e.g., finding local employment assistance) or referrals for additional services (e.g., relationship counseling). The current study focused on the latter types of calls: calls that were not simply informational or crisis situations but involved inquiry by triage consultants to identify and provide appropriate information or referrals to callers.

Call Handling Procedures

Calls to the Military OneSource call center typically begin with a request or statement by the caller and a verification of the caller's contact information and eligibility for call center services. The triage consultant then engages the caller in conversation about the topic of their inquiry. This engagement might be done relatively quickly if the caller has a straightforward issue and the referral or other solution is clear, or it might take several minutes of questioning and listening to the caller's responses to assess the nature of the caller's problem and the best service for referral. According to program guidelines, triage consultants are to be empathetic to a caller's concerns, practice active listening, validate the caller's concerns, and ensure that the caller understands the assistance provided by the consultant (e.g., the caller understands that they are receiving a referral for non-medical counseling).

Referrals are meant to directly connect the caller to the referred service or resource. Once the appropriate service to which to refer the caller is determined, the triage consultant calls the service directly, while the caller is on the line, and attempts to make a "warm handoff," where the caller is directly connected to the service by the triage consultant. If the triage consultant is unable to connect the caller to the service, the consultant will leave a message for the service with the caller's contact information, and a representative from the service is tasked with contacting the caller to deliver the service over the phone (e.g., financial counseling) or schedule an appointment for the caller to receive the service in person. Warm handoffs are meant to engage a person seeking help with the referred service (Agency for Healthcare

Research and Quality, 2019). Research demonstrates that warm hand-offs increase the utilization of referred services, including mental health services for veterans (Ader et al., 2015; Fischer et al., 2016).

Triage consultants can refer callers to services available through subject matter experts within the Military OneSource portfolio of services, to services available through DoD, or to civilian resources. The array of services available is broad, including things like assistance with spouse employment and career opportunities, tax return preparation, childcare requests, health and wellness coaching, non-medical counseling, spousal employment, financial assistance, or referrals for medical or mental health counseling.

Call Auditing

Military OneSource personnel in Military Community and Family Policy (MC&FP) routinely listen to audio recordings of calls to audit triage consultants based on whether a list of 58 quality indicators were "met," "partially met," or "not met." Items include if the triage consultant offered the participant "the opportunity to receive outreach communication" and if the notes reflect that the "triage consultant consulted with supervisory or clinical staff, if applicable." These items are helpful to ensure that consultants comply with Military OneSource contractual documentation requirements and protocols. Nine of the 58 items focus specifically on customer service to track if the triage consultant projected "a positive, welcoming attitude" and "utilized phrases and/or other verbal gestures that demonstrate military cultural competency."[1] In addition, the *Military OneSource Annual Report* provides data on caller satisfaction with various aspects of the services, based on routine caller satisfaction surveys. These use a benchmark of 92 percent for caller satisfaction and show data from fiscal year (FY) 2018 that exceeds that benchmark on all dimensions. Outside the audit tool and caller satisfaction data, little is known about the quality of calls and the extent to which consultants appropriately address callers' concerns.

---

[1]   TC Audit Tool, revised July 2018; received by the authors from MC&FP on October 16, 2018, via email.

Previous Research

Military OneSource is a unique call center because of the very broad range of resources, services, and referrals available. Call centers available to civilians have a much narrower focus, and at other call centers the information or help is typically provided directly by the call center staff who answer the phone, whereas Military OneSource triage consultants may provide direct assistance but more frequently connect or refer the caller to another resource or service. Therefore, previous research on call centers can only provide limited insights that could be applied to Military OneSource. Nevertheless, we did review some previous literature to guide our methodology.

Most previously published research literature on call center quality focuses on crisis centers fielding suicide or other urgent health matters, including prior RAND Corporation work on California crisis call centers (Ramchand et al., 2017). This and similar studies have used a variety of methods and protocols to examine call content and quality, including embedded assessments delivered by consultants (Gould, Kalafat, et al., 2007; Kalafat et al., 2007), silent monitoring by an objective rater (Mishara et al., 2007a, 2007b; Ramchand et al., 2017), follow-up assessments or interviews of the caller after some period of time (Gould, Kalafat, et al., 2007; Gould, Harris Munfakh, et al., 2012; Kalafat et al., 2007), and, more recently, ratings of chat logs (Mokkenstorm et al., 2017). Another hotline focused on sexual assault was assessed using a caller satisfaction survey (Finn, Garner, and Wilson, 2011; Finn and Hughes, 2008), as well as the call volunteer's ratings of various aspects of the call (Finn, Garner, and Wilson, 2011). Other studies have interviewed callers to helplines for breastfeeding (Rutter and Jones, 2012; Thomson et al., 2012) or problem gambling (Shandley and Moore, 2008), for example, and found that most callers were satisfied with the help they received.

There have also been a few studies published that examine commercial, nonurgent call centers. For instance, one study of an inbound retail call center showed certain "call agent behaviors" (personalization, offer of additional services, optimal rate of speech, and absence of vocalized pauses) affected subsequent intentions to repurchase the product (Pontes

In Study 2 we interviewed a separate sample of callers to explore their experiences in interacting with Military OneSource triage consultants and determine how and whether they were successfully connected to resources or services (e.g., counseling) intended to help them resolve their problem, whether they used these resources or services, and, if so, how satisfied they were with them. As described above, the groups of callers included in the interview study were slightly different from the call ratings analysis and were as follows: (1) junior enlisted personnel (in the E3–E5 pay grades) and their family members, who may have called for any reason; and (2) those who called specifically seeking a referral for non-medical counseling (individual or relationship counseling). Interviewers used a structured interview guide and coded and analyzed interview notes to identify themes.

CHAPTER TWO

Methods

Overview

We conducted two studies to evaluate the Military OneSource call center among select groups of callers requested by the sponsor. In Study 1 we conducted an analysis of call quality, call outcomes, and caller satisfaction by rating audio recordings of calls from (1) junior enlisted service members from the E3–E5 pay grades and their family members, because calls from these pay grades had been declining; (2) those calling because of a relationship problem (e.g., seeking relationship counseling), because they constitute a large portion of calls and often result in referrals to non-medical counseling; and (3) transitioning service members, because this group became eligible to use Military OneSource relatively recently and the quality of their calls had not yet been evaluated.

In Study 2 we conducted qualitative telephone interviews with a separate sample of callers (i.e., not the same callers whose call recordings were included in Study 1) to gain a deeper understanding of call experiences, the process of receiving referrals and services, and caller satisfaction. Our intention was to interview callers from the same three groups as the call ratings study (i.e., junior enlisted service members, those with relationships problems, and those transitioning out of military service). However, we were unable to interview transitioning service members due to anticipated delays in Office of Management and Budget approvals that would not fit within the project timeline. In addition, the case management system did not allow for identification of those calling about relationship problems, and thus we had to expand the interview eligibility to those who called seeking any type of non-medical counseling (individual or relationship) or a referral to the Healthy Relationships Program. The sponsor approved of these changes to the eligibility criteria for the interview study.

Study 1: Ratings of Call Audio Recordings

We obtained approvals for data transfer and data handling from the RAND Human Subjects Protection Committee and the MC&FP privacy office. ValueOptions, the contractor administering the call center, routinely requests permission to record calls for quality assurance purposes. It identified eligible calls in the prior two months through the case management system, and audio recordings were sampled by subject of call for relationship problems, or demographic group codes for junior enlisted and transitioning service members and their families. Urgent calls were excluded. This process identified potential calls by date and time stamp. The type of call was then verified by listening to the tape before transmission to RAND. Call types could overlap (e.g., a junior enlisted service member could be calling about a relationship problem), but we describe them in this report according to the category in which they were sent by ValueOptions. Thus, the calls represent a convenience sample. We requested that ValueOptions sample calls randomly and not preselect calls, but we cannot verify that the data pull was unbiased. Thus, the calls sampled may overrepresent high-quality calls and may not be representative of the general population of calls.

To ensure an appropriate sample size of calls to rate, RAND received a total of 184 recordings, with roughly equal numbers of calls among the three groups (i.e., junior enlisted service members, those with relationship problems, and those transitioning out of military service). Calls occurred between February and August 2019, and we received the data between April and August 2019 (with some replacement calls coming in September and October). Call recordings were excluded from the study if they had technological issues that made them difficult to code or if the audio recording ended before the call was completed. Due to unexpected exclusions, we received five additional calls to replace some of the calls.

The Protocol for Rating Calls
The Rating Tool

RAND developed a rating tool to document how Military OneSource triage consultants interacted with callers and track how the referral process was handled while consultants were on the phone with callers. We used a modified version of a protocol that was used for a previous RAND study assessing the quality of a suicide crisis line (Jaycox et al., 2015). The modifications made thus involved removing items that were relevant to urgent calls (not sampled in this study) through a process described below. A copy of the final rating tool can be found in Appendix A.

The Rating Procedure

Call recordings were delivered in four batches of 34 to 60 calls over four months. The first batch of calls included a combination of all three groups of interest. For the first batch, two team members dually coded 15 calls to refine the protocol. The calls were rated in three sets, with protocol refinement occurring between sets. All team members participated in discussions about initial rating discrepancies and how to best revise the protocol to make sure it was capturing relevant information. The protocol refinement phase resulted in changes related to rating item syntax, response scales, exclusion criteria, consistency of units, and formatting of the overall rating tool for ease of use. A senior researcher also listened to audio recordings of calls and verified that the correct ratings were being applied.

The remaining calls from the first batch were coded independently by two raters to measure interrater reliability, a measure of rater consistency (McHugh, 2012). The first batch had an interrater reliability kappa (K) equaling 0.858. Due to a delay in audio recording delivery, and a change in the project team, the interrater reliability procedure was repeated with a new team member. For the second batch, two team members dually rated five calls to onboard the new member and an additional 15 to measure interrater reliability. The score for the second pair was $K = 0.863$, which exceeded the accepted 0.80 standard for interrater reliability measures (McHugh, 2012). After calculation of the interrater reliability, all discrepancies were reconciled by the raters and the senior researchers, and these ratings were included in the final data set. The remaining 128 calls were divided between the two raters for independent call quality rating. After ratings were complete, the data was processed in the Stata software package. Calls were flagged for missing response items or unexpected outliers. Two team members then went through the flagged calls to resolve discrepancies and populate missing items. Figure 2.1 describes the flow of calls received, rated, and excluded by batch.

Figure 2.1
Flowchart of Call Ratings Received, Rated, and Excluded, by Group

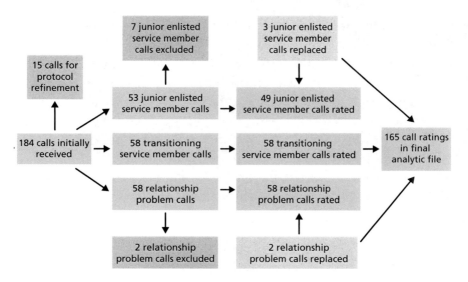

NOTE: The transitioning service member batch did not have any exclusions. Fifteen calls were used for protocol refinement, but not included in the final data set for analysis.

Study 2: Qualitative Interviews with Callers

ValueOptions was instructed to provide all callers during select weeks in May–July 2020—regardless of pay grade or reason for calling Military OneSource—with information about the study and to ask interested callers if they would give permission to have their contact information, pay grade, and the reason for their call sent to RAND. ValueOptions then sent RAND a list of all the callers who gave permission to be contacted. RAND reviewed this list and determined which callers were eligible (i.e., their pay grade was E3–E5 and/or they called seeking non-medical counseling). RAND attempted to send all eligible callers an invitation email with more information about the study. Callers who responded to this invitation email received a follow-up email with instructions for how to schedule an interview and an informed consent document to review. Participants provided verbal consent prior to beginning the interview, which lasted 15–30 minutes. Two RAND study team members conducted each interview using a structured interview guide (see Appendix B); one team member took the lead in asking questions, while the other took detailed notes (as close to a verbatim transcript as possible). These notes were coded and analyzed to identify themes. Subjective responses were double coded, and any conflicts were resolved through team discussion. The interviews were not audio recorded. After completing their interview, participants received a 20-dollar Amazon gift card via email. These procedures were approved by the RAND Human Subjects Protection Committee and the MC&FP privacy office.

Interview prompts and questions included the following:

1. how interviewees found out about Military OneSource and why they contacted the service
2. other sources they had tried to use to solve their problem prior to contacting Military OneSource
3. their general experience in talking to the Military OneSource triage consultant
4. whether they had to review their contact information and eligibility with the triage consultant and whether having to provide this information would discourage them from calling again

5. whether they would change anything about the currently available methods of connecting to Military OneSource (800 number, chat) and their opinion about potential additional connection options (e.g., social media)

6. the process of how the triage consultant connected them to resources and services, whether or not they used the referred resources/services, and, if so, whether they found them helpful

7. various ratings of their experience (e.g., positive, neutral, or negative; satisfied or unsatisfied; very helpful, somewhat helpful, or not helpful)

8. the value of Military OneSource compared with other military and civilian services

9. whether they would recommend Military OneSource to others;

10. general comments.

ValueOptions sent RAND a list of the 1,091 callers who gave permission to be contacted. After screening them for eligibility (i.e., those who were junior enlisted service members and/or called about non-medical counseling), we determined that 638 were eligible and attempted to send all 638 email invitations to participate. A very small number of eligible callers did not receive the invitation email because they did not provide a valid email address. A total of 43 callers (7 percent of those eligible) scheduled an interview, of whom 40 (6 percent of those eligible) completed the interview. Their calls to Military One-Source occurred between May 15 and July 14, 2020, and we conducted the interviews between June 3 and July 30, 2020. Notably, this timing coincided with city- and state-level restrictions in mobility and activities related to the COVID-19 pandemic. We do not know if COVID-19 affected response rates. As recommended by the sponsor, we did not alter the interview protocol to include any questions specific to COVID-19; however, if an interviewee mentioned that COVID-19 affected his or her experience, we made note of it and asked relevant follow-up questions.

CHAPTER THREE

Results

Study 1: Ratings of Call Audio Recordings

Description of Calls and Callers

We present results in this section grouped by the category they were identified in via ValueOptions. However, as can be seen in Table 3.2, there is some overlap across groups. For instance, 18 percent of junior enlisted and 29 percent of transitioning service members discussed relationship problems (as rated by our coders). Overall, rated calls exhibited few technical issues (of the nine excluded calls, eight were excluded for technical issues). It is unclear whether technical issues arose during the call between the Military OneSource triage consultant and the caller or if the issues were a result of the handling and/or processing of the audio recordings after the call was completed. Almost all recordings (99 percent) selected for rating had good sound fidelity; in fact, only one call had a technological issue affecting the ability of the Military OneSource triage consultant to communicate with the caller. In this call, the caller was disconnected for an unknown reason, but the Military OneSource triage consultant called back immediately and continued the call.

The mean call length for all calls rated was 13 minutes, 49 seconds, about the same length as the calls in earlier RAND work on crisis calls (14 minutes; Ramchand et al., 2017). The mean length of relationship calls was substantially longer than the junior enlisted or transitioning calls: about 17 and a half minutes for relationship calls compared with about 12 minutes for the other two types of calls (even though the junior enlisted service member calls and transitioning service member calls sometimes also focused on relationship problems, as will be discussed below). This may be due to the high percentage of relationship calls requesting counseling services, thus requiring a mental health screen and a joint conference call to an external provider, extending the call length. Figure 3.1 shows the average length of calls.

During 95 percent of the calls, the Military OneSource triage consultants collected contact information and eligibility information from the caller (i.e., verifying eligibility for first-time callers, validating the caller's record after a lapse of contact with Military OneSource for an extended period). On calls where this information was collected, the process on average took two minutes, 51 seconds. However, there were four calls (2 percent) where this process took between seven and ten minutes.

About one-third of callers were placed on mute for part of the call so that the triage consultant could consult with a colleague about a challenging situation. About one-fourth of callers were placed on mute once during their call; less than 5 percent of callers were placed on mute twice during their call. The average length of total time on mute during a call was two minutes. Of the individuals who were placed on mute, only 8 percent of these callers were on mute for longer than three minutes. The longest total time a caller was placed on mute was seven minutes.

Figure 3.1
Average Length of Calls, by Group, in Minutes

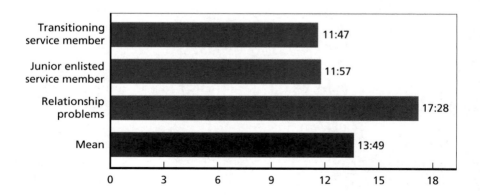

Demographics

Table 3.1 shows the general demographics of callers. Among the calls rated, the majority (about 60 percent) of callers were male, and the calls exhibited no variation across the three targeted groups regarding gender. The majority of family members who called in were women (92 percent), whereas the majority of those on active duty were men (85 percent). About one-fourth to one-third of callers were family members for relationship problem or junior enlisted member calls, whereas only 16 percent of the transitioning member calls were from family members. Unsurprisingly, due to the purposive sampling of the call groups, the large majority (84 percent) of the transitioning calls were made by service members who had already left the military (within 365 days of separation). Overall, about one in ten callers were from National Guard or reserve affiliates.

Table 3.1
Demographics of Callers (Number and Percentage of Calls), by Group

	Relationship Problems (*N* = 58)	Junior Enlisted Members (*N* = 49)	Transitioning Members (*N* = 58)	All Calls (*N* = 165)
Gender				
Male	35 (60)	29 (59)	36 (62)	100 (61)
Female	23 (40)	20 (41)	22 (38)	65 (39)
Military status				
Active duty	34 (59)	21 (43)	0 (0)	55 (33)
Family member	15 (26)	15 (31)	9 (16)	39 (24)
National Guard or reserve	7 (12)	11 (22)	0 (0)	18 (11)
Recently left military	2 (3)	2 (4)	49 (84)	53 (32)

NOTE: The calls were preselected to target the three groups, with some overlap between the groups; thus, comparisons should not be made across columns. "All Calls" data only represent the calls the team rated and may not be representative of all incoming Military OneSource calls.

Reasons for Calling

Within the calls we rated, there were often a number of different issues discussed. Because each call could contain multiple issues, the total number of problems discussed is larger than the total number of calls. For instance, a call that was selected because it included discussion of relationship problems could also include discussion of financial problems. Raters were instructed to include a topic if it was mentioned at any point in the call.

Our protocol assessed the focus of the call—that is, whether callers were seeking help for only themselves, themselves and their partners (e.g., relationship counseling), or for someone else. However, the majority of calls were related to issues affecting the callers themselves or the callers and their partners. Only four calls (2 percent) were made to get help for someone else. Thus, we collapsed these categories for the descriptions provided below and in Table 3.2.

The distribution of call types is displayed in Table 3.2. Among the calls rated, relationship problems were commonly noted as a reason for calling Military OneSource across all groups of calls. However, reasons for calling varied. Junior enlisted callers were the most likely to call for mental health issues (16 percent), and nearly one-third of junior enlisted and transitioning service member calls alike discussed financial problems.

Other reasons for calling accounted for a significant portion calls among the junior enlisted and transitioning service member groups. Since the "other" option on the call rating form was a free text response item, we reviewed and qualitatively coded the responses. Other reasons for calls were widely varied, and few themes emerged between the groups for these reasons. Of the 36 calls rated for "other," five calls requested translation services and seven were for tax or legal questions. In general, the remaining 24 calls with "other" reasons for calling requested general coaching or advice. Some examples of these reasons for calling include fitness and nutrition coaching, education consultation for a parent of a child with special needs, life coaching to improve decisionmaking skills, and advice regarding moving.

Table 3.2
Number and Percentage of Calls That Addressed Each Topic, by Group

	Relationship Problems (*N* = 58)	Junior Enlisted Members (*N* = 49)	Transitioning Members (*N* = 58)	All Calls (*N* = 165)
Relationship	56 (97)	9 (18)	17 (29)	82 (50)
Family conflict	2 (3)	1 (2)	2 (3)	5 (3)
Concern about family	1 (2)	0 (0)	2 (3)	3 (2)
Concern about friend	0 (0)	0 (0)	0 (0)	0 (0)
Work	0 (0)	2 (4)	4 (7)	6 (4)
Financial problems	1 (2)	14 (29)	17 (29)	32 (19)
Suicidal thoughts	0 (0)	0 (0)	0 (0)	0 (0)
Exposure to violence	0 (0)	0 (0)	0 (0)	0 (0)
Loss of family member	1 (2)	1 (2)	0 (0)	2 (1)
Homelessness (or fear thereof)	0 (0)	0 (0)	2 (3)	2 (1)
Alcohol and drug problems	0 (0)	0 (0)	0 (0)	0 (0)
Sexual orientation	0 (0)	0 (0)	0 (0)	0 (0)
Illness or injury	0 (0)	0 (0)	0 (0)	0 (0)
Chronic pain	0 (0)	0 (0)	1 (2)	1 (1)
Mental health (e.g., posttraumatic stress disorder [PTSD], anxiety, stress, etc.)	5 (9)	8 (16)	4 (7)	17 (10)
Medical health services	0 (0)	3 (6)	0 (0)	3 (2)
Transitioning from the military	0 (0)	3 (6)	16 (28)	19 (12)
Other	1 (2)	18 (37)	17 (29)	36 (22)

NOTE: Calls by group can sum to over 100 because some callers raised more than one problem in a single call. The calls were preselected to target the three groups, with some overlap between the groups; thus, comparisons should not be made across columns. "All Calls" data only represent the calls the team rated and may not be representative of all incoming Military OneSource calls.

Call Context

All of the calls were nonurgent, as planned. However, the degree of callers' distress varied somewhat, as can be seen in Table 3.3. Overall, the majority of the callers (65 percent) were rated as at least a little bit distressed when they described their reason for calling during the call,

Table 3.3
Context of Calls (Number and Percentage of Calls), by Group

	Relationship Problems (N = 58)	Junior Enlisted Members (N = 49)	Transitioning Members (N = 58)	All Calls (N = 165)
Rating of caller distress				
Not at all	12 (21)	19 (39)	27 (47)	58 (35)
A little	35 (60)	22 (45)	21 (36)	78 (47)
Moderately	11 (19)	7 (14)	10 (17)	28 (17)
Extremely	0 (0)	1 (2)	0 (0)	1 (1)
How challenging was the problem discussed on the call (urgent or complicated issues)?				
1—Not at all	46 (79)	37 (76)	42 (72)	125 (76)
2—	10 (17)	8 (16)	9 (16)	27 (16)
3—	2 (3)	4 (8)	7 (12)	13 (8)
4—	—	—	—	—
5—Extremely	—	—	—	—
How challenging was the caller (uncooperative, incoherent, belligerent, rejecting ideas)?				
1—Not at all	53 (91)	45 (92)	54 (93)	152 (92)
2—	5 (9)	4 (8)	2 (3)	11 (7)
3—	—	—	2 (3)	2 (1)
4—	—	—	—	—
5—Extremely	—	—	—	—

NOTE: The calls were preselected to target the three groups, with some overlap between the groups; thus, comparisons should not be made across columns.

although extreme distress was quite rare. Those calling with relationship problems were mostly rated as distressed (79 percent), and some of them began to cry during the phone calls.

Raters also gave a summary rating for how challenging the problem discussed during the call was and how challenging the caller was (e.g., uncooperative or rejecting ideas). The vast majority of calls were rated as not at all challenging, and the callers as not at all challenging.

Assessment of Communication Quality

Overall, independent raters rated the quality of communication by triage consultants during the calls as high. As is shown in Table 3.4, most ratings for positive qualities were rated as occurring "a lot," and most negative qualities were rated as occurring "not at all." These high ratings indicate very little room for improvement on the calls obtained for this study. However, two rating items (showed empathy/validated callers, explained things in a way that was easy for callers to understand) showed a little more variability for junior enlisted personnel, with about 8–10 percent of the ratings falling into the "moderately" or "a little" category rather than "a lot" (there were no ratings given in the "not at all" category).

Triage consultants were likely to be able to establish good contact and rapport with callers, and to engage in collaborative problem solving with them (see Table 3.5). In all cases, they were able to engage with callers in this way, though raters noted some weaknesses in rapport in 10 percent of calls, and some challenges in problem solving in 3 percent of calls.

Call Outcomes and Caller Satisfaction

Within the context of the calls described above, the occurrence of a warm handoff (i.e., the triage consultant connecting the caller directly to the resource/service within a three-way call) was highly variable across the calls rated. The variation is due to the type of requests fielded by Military OneSource triage consultants. Calls requesting counseling services required consultants to employ joint conference calls to providers external to OneSource, limiting the triage consultants' control over whether a warm handoff could be performed. In some instances, the triage consultant transferred the caller to other parts of Military

Table 3.4
Military OneSource Triage Consultant Communication Quality (Number and Percentage of Calls), by Group

	Relationship Problems (*N* = 58)	Junior Enlisted Members (*N* = 49)	Transitioning Members (*N* = 58)	All Calls (*N* = 165)
	A lot	**A lot**	**A lot**	**A lot**
Allowed callers to talk about their feelings/situations	55 (95)	46 (94)	57 (98)	158 (96)
Reflected back callers' feelings	54 (93)	46 (94)	55 (95)	155 (94)
Reflected back callers' situation	57 (98)	49 (100)	55 (95)	161 (98)
Connected/established rapport with callers	56 (97)	48 (98)	56 (97)	160 (97)
Overall, was sensitive/receptive to caller(s)' problems	57 (98)	48 (98)	58 (100)	163 (99)
Was respectful	58 (100)	49 (100)	56 (97)	163 (99)
Showed empathy/validated callers	56 (97)	45 (92)	58 (100)	159 (96)
Seemed knowledgeable about the callers' areas of concern	56 (97)	46 (94)	56 (97)	158 (96)
Explained things in a way that was easy for callers to understand	57 (98)	44 (90)	54 (93)	155 (94)
	Not at all	**Not at all**	**Not at all**	**Not at all**
Displayed inappropriate behavior (i.e., fell asleep, laughed at callers)	58 (100)	49 (100)	56 (97)	163 (99)
Was judgmental	58 (100)	48 (98)	58 (100)	164 (99)
Seemed to rush callers	57 (98)	48 (98)	58 (100)	163 (99)
Preached or forced opinions on callers	58 (100)	49 (100)	58 (100)	165 (100)
Was condescending	56 (97)	49 (100)	58 (100)	163 (99)
Challenged callers (in a negative way)	58 (100)	49 (100)	58 (100)	165 (100)

NOTE: Items were rated on a four-point scale: "not at all," "a little," "moderately," or "a lot." The calls were preselected to target the three groups, with some overlap between the groups; thus, comparisons should not be made across columns. "All Calls" data only represent the calls the team rated and may not be representative of all incoming Military OneSource calls.

Table 3.5
Military OneSource Triage Consultant Rapport Building and Problem
Solving (Number and Percentage of Calls), by Group

	Relationship Problems (*N* = 58)	Junior Enlisted Members (*N* = 49)	Transitioning Members (*N* = 58)	All Calls (*N* = 165)
Established good contact/ rapport				
Consistently	51 (88)	45 (92)	52 (90)	148 (90)
Some weaknesses	7 (12)	4 (8)	6 (10)	17 (10)
Did not establish	0 (0)	0 (0)	0 (0)	0 (0)
Problem solving				
Collaborative	57 (98)	46 (94)	57 (98)	160 (97)
Some weaknesses	1 (2)	3 (6)	1 (2)	5 (3)
Did not use	0 (0)	0 (0)	0 (0)	0 (0)

NOTE: The calls were preselected to target the three groups, with some overlap between the groups; thus, comparisons should not be made across columns. "All Calls" data only represent the calls the team rated and may not be representative of all incoming Military OneSource calls.

OneSource (e.g., fitness and nutrition consultation, permanent change of station [PCS] consultation, or tax and legal consultation).

Overall, triage consultants were successful in providing referrals in 99 percent of calls, and weaknesses were noted by raters in only 3 percent. Nearly all the time, triage consultants made sure all questions were answered (98 percent).

The question "How effective was this call in identifying an appropriate referral and providing referral details?" was rated on a 1 ("very ineffective intervention") to 5 ("very effective intervention") scale. The average value for relationship calls was 4.98; the average value for junior enlisted member calls was 4.92; the average value for transitioning member calls was 4.88; and the average overall score was 4.93. Of the entire set of 165 included calls, only two calls received a 3 rating; the rest were all 4 or 5 ratings.

Ratings of caller satisfaction were also high, with 93 percent rated as ending with an extremely satisfied caller, and 7 percent with a some-

Table 3.6
Call Outcomes (Number and Percentage of Calls), by Group

	Relationship Problems (*N* = 58)	Junior Enlisted Members (*N* = 49)	Transitioning Members (*N* = 58)	All Calls (*N* = 165)
Provided referrals				
Consistently	57 (98)	46 (94)	56 (97)	159 (96)
Some weaknesses	1 (2)	3 (6)	1 (2)	5 (3)
None provided	0 (0)	0 (0)	1 (2)	1 (1)
Warm handoff				
Performed	13 (22)	28 (57)	29 (50)	70 (42)
Attempted but unable	43 (74)	10 (20)	20 (34)	73 (44)
Did not attempt	1 (2)	4 (8)	5 (9)	10 (6)
Was not applicable	1 (2)	7 (14)	4 (7)	12 (7)
Made sure all questions were answered?				
Yes	58 (100)	47 (96)	57 (98)	162 (98)
How satisfied was caller?				
Not at all	0 (0)	0 (0)	1 (2)	1 (1)
Somewhat	1 (2)	3 (6)	7 (12)	11 (7)
Extremely	57 (98)	46 (94)	50 (86)	153 (93)

NOTE: Response item groups may add to over or under 100 percent due to rounding.

what satisfied caller; only 1 percent were rated as not at all satisfied. Table 3.6 shows the outcomes of the calls.

Study 2: Qualitative Interviews with Callers

Description of Calls and Demographic Characteristics of the Interviewees

As is shown in Table 3.7, about half of the interviewees (21) were service members; the remainder (19) were spouses of service members.

Table 3.7
Demographics of Callers Interviewed

	Number of Callers	Percentage of Callers
Gender		
Female	19	75
Male	10	25
Service Member or Spouse		
Service member	21	53
Spouse	19	48
Rank		
Junior enlisted member	25	63
Other	15	38
Service Branch		
Army	18	45
Navy	10	25
Air Force	10	25
Marine Corps	2	5
Method Used to Initiate Contact		
800 number	32	80
Chat	8	20
First-Time Caller		
Yes	12	30
No	28	70
Reason for Calling		
Individual counseling	19	48
Relationship counseling	10	25
Spouse Education and Career Opportunities (SECO)/MyCAA	6	15
Translation services	2	5
Other benefits	3	8

Just over half of the service members interviewed (11 out of 21) were women, and all spouses were men. As planned, over half (25) of the interviewees were junior enlisted service members or their family members. Interviewees represented all four service branches, with the largest proportion coming from the U.S. Army. Just under half (19) of the interviewees were seeking individual non-medical counseling, with another 25 percent (ten) seeking relationship counseling. Although we did not systematically track service component, some interviewees offered that information (one was affiliated with the Air Force National Guard, two with the Air Force Reserve, three with the Army National Guard, and one with the Army Reserve).

More than half of the interviewees from both the junior enlisted and other pay grades were repeat callers (i.e., had contacted Military OneSource prior to their most recent contact, which was the focus of the interview; see Table 3.8).

How Did Callers Find Out About Military OneSource?

More than half of the interviewees had contacted Military OneSource prior to their most recent contact (the focus of the interview for this study). Most of the service members originally found out about Military OneSource through the military, either while on base or from their colleagues (e.g., saw a flyer; received a pamphlet; learned about Military OneSource in a briefing, meeting, training, or a yellow ribbon event).

Table 3.8
Number of New Callers by Pay Grade

	Junior Enlisted Members N (percentage)	Other Pay Grades N (percentage)
New caller	9 (36)	3 (20)
Repeat caller	15 (60)	10 (67)
Unsure/could not remember	1 (4)	2 (13)
Total	25 (100)	15 (100)

Some statements from interviewees describe this process of finding out about Military OneSource. In the parentheses at the end of each quote, we identify the interviewee by a unique number, as well as the type of caller (service member or spouse) and the reason for their call. As one caller noted,

> It's always been one of our resources for people going through some issues, and I just kind of reached out. I Googled the number and called. Probably the first time that I heard about it was from a briefing in the military. (#36, service member, individual counseling)

Another service member said,

> They tell us about it all the time, so I just kind of knew about it. I feel like there are a lot of ads for it too; they have things in the unit, it's always on a card or handout. (#20, service member, relationship counseling)

Interviewees who were spouses of service members most commonly learned about Military OneSource through their family or friends or an internet search, and one spouse stated that she learned about it on a military Facebook page. For instance, one spouse said,

> I was trying to Google about counseling sessions in general and I Googled through the Army specifically, and Military OneSource came up, and it said that you could get counseling sessions. (#9, spouse, relationship counseling)

Did Callers Have Problems Contacting Military OneSource, and Would They Prefer Other Methods of Contact?

Most interviewees initiated contact with Military OneSource via the 800 number; only eight used the online chat option. Among those who started with the chat, four later ended up speaking to a Military OneSource triage consultant via phone, either because they experienced technical difficulties with the chat ($n = 2$) or because the triage consultant suggested they switch to the phone—for example, to obtain more details ($n = 2$). One interviewee had a particularly difficult time with the chat:

> It actually was really glitchy. It kicked me out like six times, so I had to restart the conversation with a different agent every single time. That took a while. It wasn't until I got down all of the questions they needed to ask, and I would send that in one message, and finally someone said, "Let me just call you," and they called me and got through. (#30, service member, relationship counseling)

Most interviewees were very satisfied with the current options for connecting with Military OneSource (the 800 number and chat options) and did not think that any changes or additional options were needed. Many preferred the phone because they could get answers quickly and it was convenient during times of distress. Nevertheless, they thought the chat option should be retained.

When asked specifically about whether Military OneSource should add additional options for connecting, such as social media, there were mixed reactions. Some interviewees said they probably would not use social media to connect with Military OneSource because of privacy concerns. For example,

> I don't trust social media . . . being in the military, privacy is a big thing. (#31, spouse, individual counseling)

Other interviewees suggested that social media might be useful or desirable, especially among younger service members. As one put it,

> I'm also not 18 years old, [but] social media might actually work [for younger people]. (#7, service member, individual counseling)

Other suggestions for communication options included email, an online forum, an app, and/or text messaging:

> Is email available right now? I would be interested in that. Sometimes you don't have the time to sit and wait for a response on chat. You might just want to email back and forth with someone. (#39, service member, relationship counseling)

I love text rather than a chat. If there was a way to text. They could say, "Here is a hyperlink that gives you a list of four people in your area and let us know if you get a hold of any of those people." (#16, spouse, relationship counseling)

Why Did Callers Contact Military OneSource?

By nature of our eligibility criteria and our planned sampling strategy, the most common reason for contacting Military OneSource was to obtain a referral for non-medical counseling (individual or relationship counseling). In some cases, it appeared that callers did not initially ask explicitly for a counseling referral but indicated to triage consultants that they were seeking help in coping with stress or needed "someone to talk to" and the consultant then referred them to non-medical counseling. Other reasons for calling Military OneSource included seeking information about education, scholarship, and/or career benefits via SECO/MyCAA ($n = 6$), document translation services ($n = 2$), and other benefits, such as seeking childcare ($n = 3$).

Participants sought non-medical counseling via Military One-Source for a variety of reasons (e.g., grief, infertility, relationship conflicts, and other life transitions and stressors). Some interviewees noted that they chose Military OneSource because there are significant challenges with trying to be connected to a counselor through other methods (both military and nonmilitary). One interviewee noted that one must

> jump through a lot of hoops just to see a provider. . . . You have to talk to three or four people in order to get to the provider. (#3, service member, individual counseling)

For individuals who are looking for short-term counseling as they transition through difficult times, Military OneSource likely provides an alternative to other military services that can sometimes be hindered by delays. As one interviewee noted,

> Even though I knew that I could get a referral through them [the provider on base], I knew that it would be easier to go through them [Military OneSource] than to go through my command. (#24, service member, individual counseling)

Another reason that interviewees chose Military OneSource was because TRICARE provides 12 free counseling sessions with no out-of-pocket costs for service members and their families.

Privacy and issues around word getting back to command was mentioned as another reason to utilize Military OneSource for counseling referrals. One interviewee stated,

> For me, this goes back to when I was active duty. For me, we've always been very leery about going on base for services, primarily because we know the military is small and depending on what you have going on, people are concerned that their business will get out to the command. This is a way for people to feel like they aren't going to the base but can continue to be connected and use the resource. I used it [Military OneSource] because I know that on base, they were short staffed and with COVID-19 they had a lot going on. I thought it would be quicker to get services for my kids going through Military OneSource. (#19, spouse, individual counseling)

What Other Sources of Help Did Callers Try Before Contacting Military OneSource?

More than half of the interviewees had tried other resources and services or ways of getting help prior to contacting Military OneSource, including seeking assistance through other military programs, trying self-help or self-care such as exercising or meditation, and getting advice and support from friends and family. Some interviewees tried to find information or services on their own, such as through online searches. Other interviewees said they did not try anything else prior to contacting to Military OneSource, in some cases because they had had good experiences with Military OneSource in the past. As one interviewee noted,

> I may have been able to call directly, but I enjoy calling Military OneSource because they make sure I'm connected with the people I need to speak to and it's always instant. (#2, spouse, SECO/MyCAA)

Did Callers Have a Good Experience Talking to the Triage Consultants?

There was an overwhelmingly positive response in regard to callers' general experiences in communicating with Military OneSource triage consultants. Only five interviewees rated this experience as neutral, or "fine" (rather than using a more clearly "positive" word) and none said they had a negative experience. Words that were used to describe their interactions with Military OneSource triage consultants included "pleasant," "amazing," "helpful," "friendly," "caring," "understanding," "supportive," "kind," "genuine," and "professional." Interviewees noted that triage consultants made them feel comfortable discussing personal issues. Additionally, one interviewee explained how it was a relief to have someone advocate for them:

> The representative was friendly and kept acknowledging that you have this concern and we will advocate for you. In the military you have to advocate for yourself, and it gets exhausting. Having someone I never met before—it was a relief, oh my gosh, finally somebody gets it! (#21, service member, individual counseling)

Others emphasized that the consultants were very thorough in assessing their needs and connecting them to the right services. For example,

> It was really good; the person seemed like they had a lot of experience and wanted to make sure that I wasn't randomly choosing a career or being pressured by the school and that I knew what I was doing before just diving in. They seemed to have a lot of information, and it was a little bit overwhelming, but only because I find everything new overwhelming. (#11, spouse, SECO/MyCAA)

Callers also specifically mentioned that they liked that they did not have to wait long for a Military OneSource triage consultant to answer the phone and did not have to navigate automated menus, which differed from their experiences with other call centers and services. One interviewee stated that

> [it was the] best customer service I've ever had dealing with the Army. (#13, service member, individual counseling)

Did the Review of Contact Information Discourage Callers from Calling Again?

Only three interviewees stated that they were not asked or did not remember being asked to review their contact information before the

Military OneSource triage consultant could connect them to resources and services. Among the others, none said that having to review their contact information with the Military OneSource triage consultant would discourage them from calling again. Most said this process was quick, and that they would expect to have to provide this information. Two even noted that this procedure of verifying their identity actually made them feel better or more comfortable. As one noted,

> It's helpful because it prevents other people from accessing information about you. (#8, female, spouse, junior enlisted member, Air Force, SECO/MyCAA)

One interviewee who made multiple calls in a short period of time related to the same issue indicated that he was experiencing a high level of emotional distress during his first call, so it was

> a little tough that first night to get my address out . . . [but] it wasn't a big deal [during follow-up calls]. (#13, service member, individual counseling)

Finally, one interviewee suggested that Military OneSource should find a way to automatically verify contact information (e.g., by detecting callers' phone numbers) so that callers would not have to provide this information before beginning the conversation with the triage consultant.

Were Callers Connected to the Resources and Services They Were Seeking?

Almost all interviewees were connected to the resources or services that they were seeking. For those not connected, in most cases the Military OneSource triage consultants left a message in an attempt to make a referral or connection, but the interviewees did not receive a call back. In another instance, the Military OneSource triage consultant provided a list of counselors and the interviewee called the counselors themselves but was unable to reach any of them.

The process by which triage consultants connected interviewees to resources and services varied. In many cases, the consultant attempted to connect the interviewee directly to the service (i.e., a counselor) by making a three-way call (i.e., a warm handoff). In some of these cases, the counselor answered the phone and an appointment was scheduled. In other cases, the counselor did not pick up the phone and the Military OneSource consultant left a voicemail on the interviewee's behalf. The counselor then called the interviewee directly within a few days to schedule an appointment. Other interviewees received information such as a website, phone number, or a list of counselors' names and contact information directly from the Military OneSource triage consultant. Last, a few interviewees had their call transferred directly to another department to get connected to the right resources and services.

Had Callers Used the Resources and Services Recommended by Their Triage Counselor?

More than half of the interviewees reported that they had used the resources and services that Military OneSource recommended (e.g., had at least one session with a counselor). Most interviewees who had used the recommended/referred services were satisfied with them and found them helpful.

For example, one interviewee said,

> She's very easy to talk to. I think we're going to be able to get everything we need within the ten sessions with her. (#31, spouse, individual/relationship counseling)

Another interviewee described her experience as follows:

> It's been great, bringing attention to the issues that we could improve in our communication, addressing that issue instead of personalizing it—"Oh, it's your mom." When things are stressed and there are a lot of life issues, how can we make sure to have good communication? That's been great. (#14, service member, individual counseling)

Reasons for not using the services included not yet having the opportunity (e.g., the first counseling session was scheduled for a future date), no longer needing the service because of a change in one's personal circumstances, the service not being available (e.g., because of COVID-19), and two instances in which a counselor canceled or did not show up to the scheduled appointment and the interviewee had not yet rescheduled or made an appointment with a different counselor. However, interviewees who could not or had not yet used the recommended/referred services sometimes did not necessarily blame Military OneSource. As one interviewee explained,

> That counseling person—I don't blame Military OneSource for this, but my wife and I got totally ditched. Was supposed to have a telehealth appointment. We waited for a while. We tried calling the number and they said they're on another interview. They said they would call us back, but we never heard from them again. But I don't attribute that to Military OneSource. (#3, service member, relationship counseling)

Another interviewee noted,

> I have got into contact with one of the organizations, but they weren't accepting anymore new clients because of the corona[virus] and, you know, traveling by air with pets is getting more strict. (#40, spouse, other benefits)

Is There Anything Callers Would Change About Connecting to Services?

Most interviewees reported that they would not change anything about the process by which they were connected to resources or services. Some particularly appreciated the speed and efficiency of Military OneSource (i.e., how quickly they were able to schedule an appointment). For example,

> No, it's better than on the base with TRICARE. At the [name of base] they take about a week to get you what you need, and it's not streamlined. They're all over the place and not organized. Military OneSource targets what you need immediately. People don't want the runaround. They want care right away, and Military OneSource provides that. Going to a clinic on base, you would wait a long time. (#31, spouse, individual counseling)

Some interviewees said they would have preferred to receive a complete list of counselors and their contact information directly so that they could contact the counselors themselves rather than have the Military OneSource triage consultant call for them (e.g., in a three-way call) or would have preferred to only be provided with a few names at a time. One interviewee suggested having a "self-service" option:

> If I could get a map of providers in the area. Like a Google Maps application. Or just something . . . and it might exist . . . that way, when I call them up I can already see who's in my area and I can already see who's in my area logistically. (#4, service member, relationship counseling)

Other suggestions included keeping the counselor list more up to date (i.e., making sure all counselors on the list are currently accepting new referrals from Military OneSource), providing more information about counselors (e.g., their type of degree/credentials/ license and their specialty areas), and increasing the number of counselors that accept referrals from Military OneSource. As one interviewee noted,

> If there was a way for more people to take Military OneSource insurance that would be great. . . . There is extra training that you need to do for the Military OneSource qualification, so often at a therapy office there is only a single therapist that is eligible to take the Military OneSource client. (#13, service member, individual counseling)

Did Callers Get What They Needed, and Are They Satisfied with Military OneSource?

Most interviewees were satisfied with and said they got what they needed from Military OneSource and were referred to resources and services they considered to be of high quality and/or the right fit. As one interviewee explained,

> On a scale of one to ten, pretty much a ten. When you need help, you don't want it 30 days later. And that's kind of what I'm going through. (#3, service member, individual counseling)

Another stated,

> Very satisfied because I used Military OneSource in the past for the same situation [i.e., seeking counseling] and this is the first counselor that I actually feel was perfect for me. It was on the money. So, when I talked to Military OneSource, I told them I was doing it for grieving [the loss of her mother] and she got me to a grievance counselor. (#7, service member, individual counseling)

One interviewee mentioned that she actually got even more than what she needed and was informed about resources and benefits she did not know were available:

> Because sometimes I don't necessarily ask for something, and they say something like, "Are you aware that you could get a free year of LinkedIn?" And I say, "Oh, I didn't know." And they say, "Oh, did you know we can help with your résumé?" I didn't know, and they volunteer the info and available resources. If I don't know, I can't ask. (#8, spouse, SECO/MyCAA)

In a few cases, the interviewee was not completely satisfied but did not necessarily blame Military OneSource. For example,

> The level of satisfaction from Military OneSource was definitely there. I haven't received what I wanted for that. But I can't fault Military OneSource. I have to plan to call them again. It's nothing that they've done. I think I just live in a Podunk town and no one wants to talk to anybody. (#4, service member, relationship counseling)

Another interviewee explained,

> An improvement can be made. Honestly, it took over two weeks, or close to three weeks, to get that appointment. Was that on Military OneSource's end, or was that the selection of counselors that invested in the program? Not sure who to blame. It would have been super helpful to have this counseling appointment within a week or week and a half because I was making some big life

decisions. In this instance, that service did not quite meet . . . it was null and void by the time I had the appointment. The counselor was helpful, but it was really too late to help me through the stresses of the decisionmaking. I'm skeptical of the contracted counselors. I don't blame Military OneSource. It's more about vetting the investors. (#15, spouse, individual counseling)

Overall, How Helpful Did Callers Find Military OneSource?

There was an overwhelmingly positive response to the question about how helpful Military OneSource was for interviewees; nearly all interviewees said that Military OneSource was very helpful. A few interviewees described Military OneSource as "somewhat helpful" and only one said that Military OneSource was "not helpful."

Would Callers Recommend Military OneSource to Someone Else?

All 40 interviewees said they would recommend or already have recommended Military OneSource to others. For example, one interviewee said,

> Yes, I would. I'm a staff sergeant in the Marine Corps right now. It opened my eyes to my Marines. If I have Marines underneath me, if they are having similar issues or stuff like that, to send them to [Military OneSource]. (#17, service member, individual counseling).

Another interviewee said,

> Absolutely. I actually briefed it to all of our airmen. Making sure that they know that it is always available to them and their family members. (#26, service member, other benefits)

Did Callers Describe Similar Experiences with Military OneSource on Other Calls?

Given that more than half of the interviewees were repeat callers to Military OneSource, at the end of the interview we gave them an opportunity to share additional comments they had based on their overall experience with Military OneSource beyond the most recent call that was the focus of their interview. In general, interviewees expressed very positive feelings about Military OneSource and reiterated information they had already shared earlier in the interview:

> In general, my experience has been very, very positive. I've used a lot of referral requests for taxes, veteran referral, preparing for moves. So many different services. Military OneSource has a ton of connection capacity. They're doing a great job doing a lot of different stuff. I think when you get down to a lot of specific stuff, they are ripe to be picked. For example, with taxes, they know it's tax season and they're ready. They're very prepared. (#16, spouse, relationship counseling)

> I used them before at another troubled time in my life. They're very patient and understanding. I don't know if they get trained on this or not but the customer service . . . when I called I was frustrated but they never broke and they were courteous, nice, and they were doing it as if their supervisor was right there with them. I feel like they were perfect. (#26, service member, other benefits)

One interviewee talked about difficulties in getting connected with a counselor on a previous call in April 2020 due to COVID-19 (i.e., because the Military OneSource triage consultant asked her to choose in-person or telehealth and she selected in-person but most counselors were not doing in-person counseling at that time). She suggested that callers be provided with options for both in-person and telehealth counselors. Additionally, one interviewee who had called Military OneSource many times to access different types of resources and services described some variation in experiences with different triage consultants:

> I've tapped different resources. I've been talking with a specialized career counselor who is going to help with my résumé, made me aware of career opportunities to work from home on the MySECO website. Most of the time I'm calling about something specific. . . . Sometimes I've learned that it depends on who you are talking to and you get different answers. Sometimes if it doesn't make sense or I didn't fully understand I'll call back and ask the same question. Sometimes I get the same answer and sometimes a totally different answer; it depends on the person I

get and how long they have been there and if they know the ropes and the ins and outs. It depends on who you speak to. Sometimes they haven't been there that long. The only time I've been referred out [to someone else beyond the triage consultant] is for career counseling. (#8, spouse, SECO/MyCAA)

What Did Callers See as the Value of Military OneSource Compared with Other Services?

Interviewees mentioned that Military OneSource had a number of advantages compared with other military and civilian services. First, Military OneSource triage consultants were knowledgeable about military life and available resources, and interviewees felt that the consultants truly cared about helping them:

> I am a huge supporter of what Military OneSource is doing. This chapter has been rough. In the past they have been so wonderful getting services to me as a family member and getting services to clients. They've been, overall, very quality. They may or may not know the specific ins and outs of your group within the military, but they know a little bit, and they're not know-nothing. That is super valuable. It's better than going to someone who doesn't know anything about military life. Better than going to a civilian provider and spending 90 percent of the time educating them about military life. (#16, spouse, relationship counseling)

> My experience was so positive, everything so smooth; our personalities and demeanor click, so it makes it easy and comfortable, it's wonderful. It's not a waiting game, no delays, very personal and personalized and it's not just another number. (#21, service member, individual counseling)

Many interviewees also appreciated that Military OneSource was fast with regard to both how quickly a triage consultant answered the phone and getting connected to services:

> For example, when you're used to speaking to a call center [Military OneSource], where they pick up the phone right away, you call another center and they don't pick up and you can't leave a voicemail—that's like night and day. Military OneSource really

does take care of the military and their families compared to other government agencies [state and federal]. I had to call the Department of Labor, I think it was a statewide local agency, and I couldn't get anyone to answer the phone and couldn't leave a message. I remember thinking back that Military OneSource does a great job to allow us to get in touch with them and get our needs met. (#8, spouse, SECO/MyCAA)

When my referral went through my primary care provider, it took a while. The reason I reached out to Military OneSource was because they [the primary care referral] had taken so long. With Military OneSource everything is on the spot; when you call, you're not left there to deal with it on your own. It's let's see who is in your area, let's call, let's give them 24 hours to call back, and if they don't, we'll call someone else. It's very organized, structured, left no room for things to fall through the cracks. (#19, spouse, individual counseling)

If I had gone to my [primary care manager], those referrals can take six months. But with Military OneSource it's pretty quick in getting me where I needed to go. (#1, spouse, individual counseling)

Interviewees also liked that Military OneSource was free, easy to use, and available everywhere (regardless of geographic location) 24 hours a day, seven days a week. Several interviewees used the phrase "one-stop shop" to describe Military OneSource. Other words used to describe Military OneSource were "convenient" and "comprehensive." Finally, some interviewees mentioned that Military OneSource was valuable because it provided a sense of privacy. One interviewee summed up their feelings about Military OneSource as follows:

Frankly, I think we're spoiled; I don't think that happens in the civilian sector. I've never dealt with insurance as an adult because I joined the military right out of high school. I went from my mom dealing with my insurance to the Air Force dealing with my insurance. I'm pretty sure that based on what my civilian friends tell me, they don't have that kind of experience when it comes to finding a doctor or therapist. I think it's great. (#30, service member, relationship counseling)

One interviewee wished that Military OneSource eligibility could be expanded to more veterans:

I have a lot of friends that I joined with that are now out of the military; they've been out for, like, two years but the cutoff for veterans to use this [Military OneSource 800] number is, like, nine months or a year, and they are going through a lot. No one is really sure if they are eligible for that line. That's just disappointing. My experience was as good as I could possibly have hoped it to be. Really, the only thing I would change is the eligibility: it's kind of crappy that once you're out of the military you're kind of on your own. It's really hard to adjust to civilian life, and a lot of guys can't. Having a resource like this could save a lot of lives. (#13, service member, individual counseling)

What Other Comments Did Callers Have?

At the end of the interviews, interviewees had an opportunity to provide additional comments that they hadn't already shared. A couple of interviewees mentioned aspects of their experience that did not go particularly well, even if these aspects were not the fault of Military OneSource. For instance, one interviewee discussed how they would have liked to be seen by a counselor sooner but speculated that it was likely due to COVID-19. Another interviewee described a negative experience with the first counselor that she and her husband were connected to through Military OneSource; she called again to get a referral to a different counselor. One interviewee suggested that Military OneSource should emphasize trustworthiness and privacy when advertising its resources and get more military leaders on board to inform service members about the service (a "top-down" approach). Finally, other feedback included sending surveys by text and sending email summaries of what was discussed during the call. As one interviewee noted,

It was just a really good experience. It would just be great to have an email or summary of what was discussed—the numbers and the resources that were discussed. (#12, spouse, other benefits)

Some interviewees used the time at the end of the interview to reiterate the positive overall experience they had with Military One-Source, with one sharing that the service had such a positive impact on her that she is considering becoming a Military OneSource triage consultant herself:

> I think I've said it all: it's a phenomenal program, and I think it needs to keep going. (#17, service member, individual counseling)

> I think the Military OneSource is a value-added program and I would beseech anyone who controls the funding to continue funding it; don't get rid of it. (#14, service member, individual counseling)

> When I called I was near tears, frustrated, and didn't know what to do. We came here during the pandemic and didn't know what to do. I'm trying to become a teacher, and I actually started to try to learn how to become one of the representatives at Military OneSource because that's the kind of impact that they've had on me. (#26, service member, other benefits)

CHAPTER FOUR

Summary and Recommendations

Across both studies (ratings of call audio recordings and interviews with callers), we found that the calls examined in this study were almost universally of high quality with regard to communication with Military OneSource triage consultants, and callers were satisfied with their experience with the call center and were directed to resources and services they perceived as valuable and helpful. There were only a few areas that suggested room for improvement in call handling and referrals. However, there are also important limitations to the study that should be considered when interpreting the results.

Summary of Call Ratings Results

Overall, among the calls we rated, the communication quality was very high. For the vast majority of calls, the triage consultants were responsive to the callers' needs, patient with callers, and respectful. Triage consultants were also rated as knowledgeable for almost all calls, and the incidence of triage consultant negative behaviors was practically nonexistent. Although ratings of the extent to which triage consultants explained things in a way that was easy for the caller to understand were generally high, ratings were somewhat lower for junior enlisted callers. Whereas we cannot compare across the groups sampled in this study, the descriptive statistics show call quality and outcomes within each group. Around 90 percent of the content of calls from junior enlisted service members or their families were rated being explained in a way that was easy for the caller to understand "a lot": this measure was 98 percent for those calling about relationship issues and 93 percent for those transitioning out of the service. Similarly, only 92 percent of calls from junior enlisted personnel were rated as showing empathy/validating caller "a lot." It is unclear how these two ratings compare overall with callers from higher pay grades, and 90–92 percent of calls rated at the highest level is not necessarily a cause for concern. However, Military OneSource call center supervisors might review the communication training provided to triage consultants to ensure that it takes into consideration the communication patterns of diverse callers, including younger service members and their families.

Our ratings of the context of the calls reflected that while no calls were considered urgent, the level of distress experienced by callers varied quite a bit. Relationship and junior enlisted member calls were most likely to be rated as displaying some level of distress. Still, the call context was not rated as being particularly challenging, with average ratings close to a rating of "not at all challenging."

Call outcomes were positive, but there were small issues that might suggest room for improvement. Almost all consultants engaged in collaborative problem solving with callers and consistently provided referrals. Not all referrals were conducted as warm handoffs (i.e., the triage consultant connecting the caller directly to the resource/service via a three-way call): 42 percent of calls in the study involved completed warm handoffs, but another 44 percent attempted a warm handoff that was not successful (e.g., the consultant called a non-medical counselor to schedule an appointment, but the counselor's office did not pick up). Prevalence of warm handoffs seemed to differ by the reason for the call, but the differences in issues discussed across groups makes it difficult to interpret these differences. Notably, around 90 percent of calls were rated as consistently establishing good rapport between consultants and callers. Program staff should consider whether it is concerning that the 10 percent of calls were rated as having "some weaknesses." Similarly, although the vast majority of callers across groups were rated as being extremely satisfied with the call, a lower proportion of transitioning callers (86 percent) were rated as extremely satisfied, with 12 percent rated as "somewhat satisfied" and 2 percent rated as "not at all satisfied."

Summary of Caller Interview Results

Overall, interviewees conveyed that they were very satisfied with their experience in communicating with Military OneSource triage consultants. The consultants were described as friendly, supportive, helpful, and knowledgeable about military life. Interviewees indicated that Military OneSource offered significant value compared with other call centers and services, including those in the civilian community (e.g., other options for counseling, or calling other government agencies and businesses), in that Military OneSource was free, fast (with regard to how quickly consultants answered the phone and connected callers to resources and services), easy to use, available everywhere at all times, and confidential. One interviewee recommended that Military OneSource send callers an email summary of what was discussed, including contact information for any referred counselors or services, after the call.

Most interviewees said that they were successfully connected to the resources or services they were seeking, satisfied with the process used to connect them (e.g., a warm handoff or other method) and, among those who had the opportunity to use these resources/services by the time of their interviews, most said they were satisfied with the help they received. A few interviewees experienced delays in scheduling appointments or had other problems (e.g., they did not like the first counselors they saw) but did not necessarily fault the Military OneSource triage consultants.

Interviewees who were seeking non-medical counseling described Military OneSource's typical process for arranging counseling referrals as connecting the caller directly to a counselor in a three-way call (a warm handoff) or leaving a voicemail on the caller's behalf if the counselor did not answer the phone. Some interviewees expressed that they would have preferred to receive a list of counselors to contact on their own. Other suggestions included keeping the counselor list more up to date (i.e., making sure all counselors on the list are currently accepting new referrals from Military OneSource), providing more information about counselors (e.g., their type of degrees/licenses and their specialty areas), and increasing the number of providers that accept referrals from Military OneSource.

Important Limitations to the Study

Limitations to Study 1, Ratings of Call Audio Recordings

Limitations of this work include the small sample of calls that were rated ($N = 165$), in contrast to the high volume of calls that occur each month (around 32,000 calls). Thus, it is quite possible that sampled calls are not fully representative of typical calls. We were also unable to directly compare the three groups of interest (junior enlisted service members, those with relationship problems, and those transitioning out of military service) because the groups overlapped (i.e., some of the calls we rated fit into more than one group). Moreover, we did not have control over audio recording selection, and thus it is possible that there was bias in that selection. For instance, very short calls were not included, and a short call could indicate a difficulty in communication or rapport very early in a call. Moreover, there are incentives for ValueOptions to perform well, and these incentives might have produced some bias in the selection of calls. In addition, this study looked across call centers and triage consultants and did not examine differences among locations and individuals; this could obscure important variations in call quality. Among those in the transitioning group, the majority (84 percent) had already separated from the military, and thus we have less information about calls from service members or their families who are soon to transition out of the military and/or are seeking assistance from Military OneSource specifically related to transitioning. Finally, we were not able to measure follow-up on the referrals offered, or how satisfied the callers were with these referrals and the help they provided. Our telephone interviews partially addressed follow-up and satisfaction with referrals, but also had limitations that affect interpretation of the findings.

Limitations to Study 2, Qualitative Interviews with Callers

The small sample size and inability to compare subgroups due to overlap was a limitation for both the call ratings and the interviews; the sample size for callers who were interviewed ($N = 40$) is not likely to be representative of all callers. This limits our ability to make conclusions about the population of callers represented in the interviews (i.e., junior enlisted callers and those referred to non-medical counseling). In addition, as has been noted, the time needed to obtain Office of Management and Budget approvals to interview service members and their families who had transitioned out of the military precluded us from interviewing callers from that population. As with the call ratings, we did not have control over which callers were invited to participate in the interviews, and it is possible that callers perceived to be dissatisfied might not have been asked if they would provide their contact information to RAND. Furthermore, the data that ValueOptions provided did not include anything about caller satisfaction; therefore, we were unable to try to oversample callers who had negative experiences and we believe it is likely that we were unable to capture some callers who had negative experiences. Correspondingly, caller rate of agreement to be contacted for the study is unknown, so we cannot assess the potential bias in selection for participation. Additionally, many eligible callers who agreed to be contacted did not respond to RAND's email and never scheduled an interview: 40 out of 638 eligible callers were interviewed (6 percent). This relatively low response rate creates the possibility for additional bias in the sample of callers interviewed. For example, those who agreed to be contacted and actually scheduled and completed an interview might have been a subsample of callers who were particularly positive about Military OneSource, and our sample may also overrepresent female callers. Finally, as with the call ratings study, the callers were recruited for interviews across call centers and triage consultants, and the study did not examine differences among these locations and individuals. This could obscure important variations in caller experiences.

Recommendations

First, although the overall results from both studies were positive, the findings revealed some possible changes to call center operations and areas for future study. Our recommendations are as follows:

Military OneSource call center supervisors should review their existing triage consultant trainings and determine whether additional training focused on communicating with diverse service members and their families is warranted, with a particular focus on communication with junior enlisted service members.

Although ratings of the extent to which triage consultants "explained things in a way that was easy for the caller to understand" were generally high, ratings were somewhat lower for junior enlisted callers.

MC&FP should bolster and expand its advertising of Military OneSource, including emphasizing the confidentiality of the service in advertising and encouraging military leadership to publicize the service among their service members and families.

Although service members reported learning about Military OneSource through military sources, many spouses reported learning about the call center through word of mouth or internet searches. In addition, one caller suggested that military leaders should help advertise the program as a resource for service members and their families, and another caller commented that advertising should emphasize the trustworthiness and privacy provided by Military OneSource.

To improve caller utilization of programs or resources provided during the call, MC&FP should deliver postcall email summaries to callers.

Information provided during health consultations can be difficult for people to remember, and postcall summaries of topics discussed, referrals, and recommendations can help people remember the information conveyed during the consultation (Watson and McKinstry, 2009). Indeed, one caller who was interviewed suggested that it would be useful to receive a follow-up email after the call with Military OneSource that would include a summary of the call and referrals or resources recommended by the triage consultant.

Military OneSource should provide callers seeking non-medical counseling with a list of counselors in their geographic area, including the counselors' types of degrees/licenses and their areas of specialization. Similarly, Military OneSource could take steps to ensure that its list of counselors is up to date and that counselors on the list are available to take new clients.

Interviewees suggested that receiving a counselor list would allow callers to contact several counselors in their area without having to call Military OneSource again to obtain contact information for additional counselors. Callers might want to contact several counselors to see if certain ones are a better match for them, and listing the counselors' areas of specialization would allow callers to choose which ones to contact based on their needs (e.g., relationship counseling or financial issues).

A few callers had difficulty finding a counselor that was accepting new clients. Although these callers did not seem to blame Military OneSource for this problem, it could serve as a barrier to receiving counseling for some callers and could also discourage them from using Military OneSource in the future.

MC&FP should monitor and address technical difficulties that arise with using the chat function.

A few interviewees mentioned that technical issues arose when contacting triage consultants using the chat function on the Military OneSource website.

MC&FP should study the feasibility and impact of extending Military OneSource call center services to veterans beyond one year after discharge.

In the call ratings study, only 86 percent of transitioning service members were rated as extremely satisfied compared with other callers. These ratings, though very good, should be further investigated through surveys or interviews with transitioning callers. Since, as we noted in Study 1, the majority of transitioning service members have already left the military, it may be harder for triage consultants to link them to needed services in the civilian sector. In addition, although Study 2 was unable to contact transitioning callers who had already left the service, one caller who was in the process of transitioning to veteran status suggested that Military OneSource services would be helpful to them beyond one year after discharge.

Additional research would complement the present study and extend findings.

Additional research that reduces potential bias in the calls evaluated would be helpful to ensure the validity of these findings. For example, MC&FP should consider conducting a survey where respondents could be randomly sampled from the population of callers. This would allow for oversampling of callers from specific groups (e.g., new callers, men) and the results could be weighted to be representative of the population of callers. This would allow for comparisons across groups in order to understand differences in call quality, call outcomes, and caller satisfaction across subgroups, which was not possible in the present study. Examination of call quality in relation to callers' levels of distress could also be helpful. Finally, it could be helpful to bolster samples in future studies to include more variety in reasons for calling (e.g., calls about financial issues or a spouse's employment/career, which greatly increased in August 2018 when eligibility was expanded to veterans and their family members) and include more military service members and their families who are preparing to separate from the military and/or who call specifically seeking assistance related to preparing for transition, since those callers were not interviewed in this study and may benefit from the use of Military OneSource services as part of their preparation to transition.

Conclusions and Next Steps

Overall, the findings of these studies suggest that the Military One-Source calls we rated were of high quality and callers were satisfied with their experience and were directed to valuable and helpful services. Results suggest that any mildly problematic issues that were revealed in the study occurred among a small minority of callers, and program staff could assess whether these issues are of concern. However, these findings must be interpreted with caution due to the significant limitations of both studies, and especially the small sample sizes, as the samples were not selected to be representative of Military OneSource callers as a whole or their particular subgroup of callers (i.e., junior enlisted members, those with relationship problems, or those transitioning out of the military). Additional research would be needed to assess the rates of problematic issues in the population of Military OneSource callers, to compare subgroups, and to evaluate potential moderators of call outcomes and caller satisfaction, such as callers' levels of distress.

Call Rating Protocol

Call ID Number: _____

Duration: _____ (minutes)

Call Rater Initials: _____

Section A: Call Characteristics

1. **Technical/other problems resulted in abrupt termination of call?**

   _____ Yes   _____ No   (if yes, select all that apply)

	Check
1a. Counselor/caller unable to hear each other (i.e., static, noise)	
1b. Caller had to hang up (i.e., someone walked in, told to get off telephone, "have to go now")	
1c. Cell or portable telephone problems (no battery charge left/ losing service)	
1d. Other (specify):	

2. **Were there difficulties in hearing the call (connection problems, accent, etc.)?**

   _____ Yes   _____ No

3. **Caller put on mute or hold?**

_____ Yes

If "yes," how many times? _____

If "yes," for how long? _____ (min)

_____ No

4. **Caller's gender?** _____ Male   _____ Female
   _____ Don't Know

5. **Military status?**

_____ Active Duty

_____ Reserve

_____ National Guard

_____ Recently retired/honorably discharged

_____ Family member

6. **Was call selected for rating (no exclusions below)?**

_____ Yes   _____ No

Type of exclusion	Check
6a. Consultant not eligible to be silent monitored—DO NOT RATE	
6b. Did not provide consent; asked that the call not be monitored for quality or research purposes—DO NOT RATE	
6c. Lacked the capacity to give consent (e.g., in midst of psychotic episode or exhibiting dementia or so intoxicated/high that it interfered with communication)—DO NOT RATE	
6d. Minor (less than 18 years of age)—DO NOT RATE	
6e. Call not in English—DO NOT RATE (which language, if known):	
6f. Obscene/prank caller—DO NOT RATE	
6g. Very short "Quick Tracker" type information-only call— DO NOT RATE	
6h. Follow-up call to provide additional information/referral— DO NOT RATE	
6i. Other (specify):	

7. **Did this call include contact information and eligibility determination (i.e., first-time caller, validating record after extended period)?**

_____ Yes

If yes, how long did this process take? _____ (min)

_____ No

Brief Summary of Call: _____

_____

Section B: Call Content

Check all that apply:

	Problem for caller	Problem for someone else	Problem for both
1. Relationship problems (e.g., partner)			
2. Family conflict problems (not partner)			
3. Concern about a family member			
4. Concern about a friend			
5. Work problems (e.g., unemployment, issues at work)			
6. Financial problems (e.g., no money, needs money, pension problems, disability stopped)			
7. Suicidal thoughts/intent (including current, past, or worry about potential of future thoughts or intent)			
8. Exposure to violence or trauma (or fear of)			
9. Loss of family member/friend (e.g., grief)			
10. Homelessness (or fear of)			
11. Alcohol/drug use problems (current)			
12. Sexual orientation problems			

	Problem for caller	Problem for someone else	Problem for both
13. Illness/injury/disability problems (physical health)			
14. Chronic pain (from illness or injury)			
15. Depression/anxiety/PTSD/other mental health problem (e.g., states concern about experiencing symptoms [sleeplessness, memory loss, hearing voices, confusion])			
16. Getting medical/mental health services			
17. Transition out of the military			
18. Other (specify):			

Section C: Telephone Counselor Response

	Not at all or Not applicable (0)	A little (1)	Moderately (2)	A lot (3)
1. Allowed caller(s) to talk about his/her feelings/situation?				
2. Reflected back caller(s)' feelings?				
3. Reflected back caller(s)' situation?				
4. Connected/established rapport with caller(s)				
5. Overall, was sensitive/receptive to caller(s)' problems				
6. Was respectful				
7. Showed empathy/validated caller(s)				
8. Seemed knowledgeable about the caller(s)' area of concern				
9. Explained things in a way that was easy for the caller to understand				

	Not at all or Not applicable (0)	A little (1)	Moderately (2)	A lot (3)
10. Displayed inappropriate behavior (i.e., fell asleep, laughed at caller[s])				
11. Was judgmental				
12. Seemed to rush the caller				
13. Preached or forced his/her opinions on caller(s)				
14. Was condescending				
15. Challenged caller(s) (in a negative way)				

Section D: Distress During Call

	Not at all distressed (0)	A little distressed (1)	Moderately distressed (2)	Extremely distressed (3)
Rate the level of distress of the CALLER (based on tone and affect) when describing the problem				

Section E: Overall Ratings *(code based on everyone triage consultant spoke with)*

1. **Good contact/rapport** *(check one item)*

   a. _____ Established good contact/rapport (consistently understood and connected)

   b. _____ Established good contact/rapport with some weaknesses (had a few times where the consultant did not understand or connect)

   c. _____ Did not establish good contact/rapport, or important weaknesses (did not seem to connect or understand, made the caller or someone else upset or shut down)

2. **Problem solving** *(check one item)*

   a. _____ Collaborative problem-solving approach used (consistently offered choices and options and asked for input)

   b. _____ Collaborative problem-solving approach used, with some weaknesses (came up with Military OneSource ideas for the plan, did not check on all parts of the plan)

   c. _____ Did not use collaborative problem-solving approach, or had important weaknesses (suggested a plan without input, did not seem to have caller agreement on plan)

3. **Referrals** *(check one item) NOTE these include both within OneSource and to outside entities*

   a. _____ Referrals/resources provided (consistently checked on types of referrals needed or desired and whether referrals were satisfactory)

   b. _____ Referrals/resources provided with some weaknesses or incomplete (addressed some but not all problems, did not check on all referrals to see if they were satisfactory)

   c. _____ No referrals/resources provided, or important weaknesses (e.g., did not offer referrals or resources at all, or gave information without checking on whether any of it would be helpful or useful)

4. **Warm handoff** *(check one item) NOTE these include both within OneSource and to outside entities*

   a. _____ Consultant was able to make a warm handoff with the referral or Military OneSource specialist for at least one problem (e.g., speak with someone on a three-way call to set up an appointment)

   b. _____ Consultant attempted a warm handoff for at least one problem, but it was not successful (initiated a three-way call but got an answering machine and left a message)

   c. _____ No warm handoff attempted (consultant gave a phone number to the caller)

   d. _____ Not applicable (no referral made)

5. **This call can be classified as:**

   Urgent

   Nonurgent

6. **If URGENT: How effective was this call in making the caller (or person at risk) safe?**

   (circle one or leave blank)

Very Ineffective Intervention				Very Effective Intervention
1	2	3	4	5

7. **If NONURGENT: How effective was this call in identifying an appropriate referral and providing referral details?**

   (circle one or leave blank)

Very Ineffective Intervention				Very effective Intervention
1	2	3	4	5

8. **How challenging was the situation on this call (e.g., urgent or complicated issues)?**

   (circle one)

Not at All Challenging				Extremely Challenging
1	2	3	4	5

9. **How challenging was/were caller(s) (e.g., uncooperative, incoherent, belligerent, rejects ideas)?**

   (circle one)

Not at All Challenging				Extremely Challenging
1	2	3	4	5

10. **Did the consultant make sure all questions were answered?**

    Yes / No

11. **How satisfied was/were caller(s) at the end of the call?**

Not at All Satisfied	Somewhat Satisfied	Extremely Satisfied
1	2	3

Interview Questions

Demographic Information

1. Are you a service member or the family member of someone who serves?
   a. *If family member:* What is your relationship with your service member sponsor?

2. What is your [your family member's] service?
   a. (Army, Navy, Marine Corps, Air Force, Coast Guard)

3. What is your [your family member's] rank or pay grade?

Experiences and Engagement with Military OneSource

4. How did you find out about the Military OneSource call center?
   a. Have you used the call center before?
   b. Did you call the 800 number, or use the chat function?

5. What prompted you to contact Military OneSource in the first place?
   a. *Probe (if not clear):* Generally, what type of challenge were you experiencing?

6. What else had you tried to solve your problem?
   a. *Probe (if not clear):* Where these military services or programs?

7. What was your experience talking to the call center representative?
    a. *Probe (if not clear):* Did you face any challenges interacting with them?

8. Did you have to review your contact information and eligibility with the call center representative?
    If yes:
    a. How long did that take?
    b. Would having to provide this information discourage you from calling again?

9. Would you change anything about how you connect to Military OneSource consultants?

10. Are there other ways you would like to connect with Military OneSource consultants (e.g., through social media)?

Connecting to Resources

11. What kind of help were you hoping to get by contacting Military OneSource?
    a. *Probe (if needed):* Were you looking for basic information? Advice? A referral to another program?

12. Was the call center able to connect you to these resources?
    If no:
    a. Did someone follow up and connect you with the resource later?
        a-1. *If no:* Did you try to connect to the resource on your own?
    b. Were you satisfied with the call center's help in connecting you?
    c. What else could the call center have done to connect you with resources?
    If yes:
    d. How did they connect you to the resource?
        d-1. *Probe (if not clear):* Did the call center provide you with contact information or stay on the line with you?

13. Do you feel like you got what you needed from Military One-Source?
    a. Why or why not?

14. Was your experience connecting to resources and services positive, negative, or neutral?

15. Would you change anything about how you can connect to resources through the call center?

Use of Referrals

16. Were you able to use the resources/receive services that Military OneSource recommended?

    If no:
    a. What kept you from using the resources/services?

    If yes:
    b. Have the resources/services helped you so far?
    c. Do you feel like you were referred to the right resources/services to fit your needs?
    d. Were the resources high quality?
    e. Overall, how satisfied were you with the resources you were referred to?

Wrap-up

17. Overall, how helpful was the Military OneSource call center? Would you say that it was very helpful, somewhat helpful, or not helpful?

18. What do you see as the value in Military OneSource compared with other services, including those in the civilian community?

19. Would you recommend Military OneSource to someone else?

20. Do you have anything else that you would like to share with us?

References

Ader, Jeremy, Christopher J. Stille, David Keller, Benjamin F. Miller, Michael S. Barr, and James M. Perrin, "The Medical Home and Integrated Behavioral Health: Advancing the Policy Agenda," *Pediatrics*, Vol. 135, No. 5, 2015, pp. 909–917.

Agency for Healthcare Research and Quality, *Implementation Quick Start Guide: Warm Handoff*, Rockville, Md.: Agency for Healthcare Research and Quality, 2019. As of July 3, 2019:
https://www.ahrq.gov/sites/default/files/wysiwyg/professionals/quality-patient-safety/patient-family-engagement/pfeprimarycare/warm-handoff-qsg-brochure.pdf

Finn, Jerry, Michelle D. Garner, and Jen Wilson, "Volunteer and User Evaluation of the National Sexual Assault Online Hotline," *Evaluation and Program Planning*, Vol. 34, No. 3, 2011, pp. 266–272.

Finn, Jerry, and Penelope Hughes, "Evaluation of the RAINN National Sexual Assault Online Hotline," *Journal of Technology in Human Services*, Vol. 26, Nos. 2–4, 2008, pp. 203–222.

Fischer, Ellen P., Jean C. McSweeney, Patricia B. Wright, Ann M. Cheney, Geoffrey M. Curran, Kathy Henderson, and John C. Fortney, "Overcoming Barriers to Sustained Engagement in Mental Health Care: Perspectives of Rural Veterans and Providers," *Journal of Rural Health*, Vol. 32, No. 4, 2016, pp. 429–438.

Gould, Madelyn S., Jimmie L. Harris Munfakh, Marjorie Kleinman, and Alison M. Lake, "National Suicide Prevention Lifeline: Enhancing Mental Health Care for Suicidal Individuals and Other People in Crisis," *Suicide and Life-Threatening Behavior*, Vol. 42, No. 1, 2012, pp. 22–35.

Gould, Madelyn S., John Kalafat, Jimmie Lou Harris Munfakh, and Marjorie Kleinman, "An Evaluation of Crisis Hotline Outcomes, Part 2: Suicidal Callers," *Suicide and Life-Threatening Behavior*, Vol. 37, No. 3, 2007, pp. 338–352.

Jaycox, Lisa H., Rajeev Ramchand, Patricia A. Ebener, Dionne Barnes-Proby, and Marylou Gilbert, *RAND's Silent Monitoring Protocol for Assessing Suicide Crisis Line Call Content and Quality*, Santa Monica, Calif.: RAND Corporation, TL-150-CMHSA, 2015. As of November 17, 2020: https://www.rand.org/pubs/tools/TL150.html

Kalafat, John, Madelyn S. Gould, Jimmie Lou Harris Munfakh, and Marjorie Kleinman, "An Evaluation of Crisis Hotline Outcomes, Part 1: Nonsuicidal Crisis Callers," *Suicide and Life-Threatening Behavior*, Vol. 37, No. 3, 2007, pp. 322–337.

McHugh, Mary L., "Interrater Reliability: The Kappa Statistic," *Biochemia Medica*, Vol. 22, No. 3, 2012, pp. 276–282.

Military OneSource, *Military OneSource Annual Report 29 November 2018*, unpublished annual report provided by U.S. Department of Defense to the RAND Corporation.

Mishara, Brian L., François Chagnon, Marc Daigle, Bogdan Balan, Sylvaine Raymond, Isabelle Marcoux, and Alan Berman, "Comparing Models of Helper Behavior to Actual Practice in Telephone Crisis Intervention: A Silent Monitoring Study of Calls to the US 1-800-SUICIDE Network," *Suicide and Life-Threatening Behavior*, Vol. 37, No. 3, 2007a, pp. 291–307.

———, "Which Helper Behaviors and Intervention Styles Are Related to Better Short-Term Outcomes in Telephone Crisis Intervention? Results from a Silent Monitoring Study of Calls to the US 1-800-SUICIDE Network," *Suicide and Life-Threatening Behavior*, Vol. 37, No. 3, 2007b, pp. 308–321.

Mokkenstorm, Jan K., Merijn Eikelenboom, Annemiek Huisman, Jasper Wiebenga, Renske Gilissen, Ad J. F. M. Kerkhof, and Johannes H. Smit, "Evaluation of the 113Online Suicide Prevention Crisis Chat Service: Outcomes, Helper Behaviors and Comparison to Telephone Hotlines," *Suicide and Life-Threatening Behavior*, Vol. 47, No. 3, 2017, pp. 282–296.

Office of People Analytics, *2017 Survey of Active Duty Spouses: Tabulations of Responses*, Alexandria, Va.: Office of People Analytics, 2018.

Pontes, Manuel C. F., and Colleen O'Brien Kelly, "The Identification of Inbound Call Center Agents' Competencies That Are Related to Callers' Repurchase Intentions," *Journal of Interactive Marketing*, Vol. 14, No. 3, 2000, pp. 41–49.

Rafaeli, Anat, Lital Ziklik, and Lorna Doucet, "The Impact of Call Center Employees' Customer Orientation Behaviors on Service Quality," *Journal of Service Research*, Vol. 10, No. 3, 2008, pp. 239–255.

Ramchand, Rajeev, Lisa Jaycox, Pat Ebener, Mary Lou Gilbert, Dionne Barnes-Proby, and Prodyumna Goutam, "Characteristics and Proximal Outcomes of Calls Made to Suicide Crisis Hotlines in California," *Crisis*, Vol. 38, No. 1, 2017, pp. 26–35.

Rutter, Paul M., and Wendy Jones, "Enquiry Analysis and User Opinion of the Drugs in Breastmilk Helpline: A Prospective Study," *International Breastfeeding Journal*, Vol. 7, No. 1, 2012, p. 6.

Shandley, Kerrie, and Susan Moore, "Evaluation of Gambler's Helpline: A Consumer Perspective," *International Gambling Studies*, Vol. 8, No. 3, 2008, pp. 315–330.

Thomson, Gill, Nicola Crossland, Fiona Dykes, and Chris J. Sutton, "UK Breastfeeding Helpline Support: An Investigation of Influences upon Satisfaction," *BMC Pregnancy and Childbirth*, Vol. 12, 2012.

Trail, Thomas E., Laurie T. Martin, Lane F. Burgette, Linnea Warren May, Ammarah Mahmud, Nupur Nanda, and Anita Chandra, *An Evaluation of U.S. Military Non-Medical Counseling Programs*, Santa Monica, Calif.: RAND Corporation, RR-1861-OSD, 2017. As of November 18, 2020: https://www.rand.org/pubs/research_reports/RR1861.html

Watson, Philip W. B., and Brian McKinstry, "A Systematic Review of Interventions to Improve Recall of Medical Advice in Healthcare Consultations," *Journal of the Royal Society of Medicine*, Vol. 102, No. 6, 2009, pp. 235–243.